YOUNG ARTIST SERIES

LEARN TO DRAW... PETS!

By Mara Conlon

Illustrated by Kerren Barbas Steckler

Designed by Heather Zschock

PETER PAUPER PRESS, INC.
Rye Brook, New York

For Copeland, Emily, Audrey, Jake, Robin, Max, and the Scarly Squad

PETER PAUPER PRESS

In 1928, at the age of twenty-two, Peter Beilenson began printing books on a small press in the basement of his parents' home in Larchmont, New York. Peter—and later, his wife, Edna—sought to create fine books that sold at "prices even a pauper could afford."

Today, still family owned and operated, Peter Pauper Press continues to honor our founders' legacy of quality, value, and fun for big kids and small kids alike.

Designed by Heather Zschock

Manufactured for Peter Pauper Press, Inc.
3 International Drive
Rye Brook, NY 10573 USA

ISBN 978-1-4413-3129-8
Printed in China

Published in the United Kingdom and Europe by
Peter Pauper Press, Inc. c/o White Pebble International
Unit 2, Plot 11 Terminus Road
Chichester, West Sussex PO19 8TX, UK

7 6 5

Are you ready to learn how to draw 43 different cats, dogs, bunnies and other terrific pets? It's easy and fun! Just follow these steps:

First, pick a cat, dog, or other pet you want to draw.

Next, trace over the picture with a pencil. This will give you a feel for how to draw the lines.

Then, following the numbers, start drawing each new step **(shown in red)** of the picture in the empty space in each scene, or on a piece of paper. Some pictures will have you start out by drawing some basic shapes to use as guidelines. When you are finished with your drawing, erase these gray lines.

Lastly, if you're an awesome artist (and of course, you are!), try drawing a whole scene with one or more of the pets in this book. And remember, don't worry if your drawings look different from the ones in this book—no two pets are exactly alike!

You're on your way to creating your own special masterpieces!

GET READY! GET SET! DRAW!

Cat
1.
To begin: Lightly draw these basic shapes.
2.
Then: Follow each new step in red to draw this cat.
3.
4.
5.
6.
Persian Cat
1.
To begin: Lightly draw these basic shapes.
2.
Then: Follow each new step in red to draw this persian cat.
3.
4.
5.
6.

Trace over us
for practice!

Golden Retriever

1. **To begin:** Lightly draw these basic shapes.

2. **Then:** Follow each new step in red to draw this golden retriever.

3.

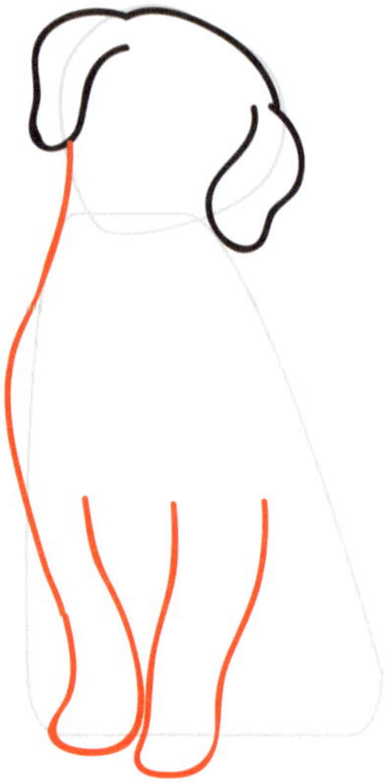

4.

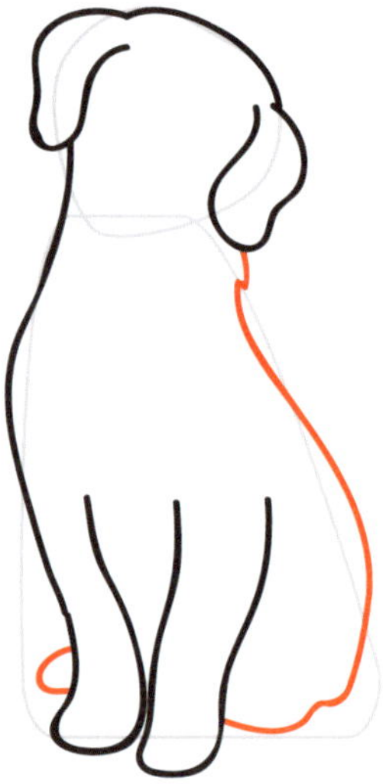

5.

6.

Dachshund

1. **To begin:** Lightly draw these basic shapes.

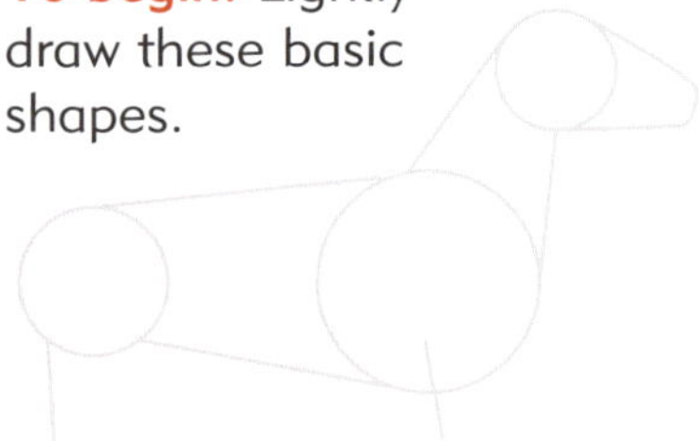

2. **Then:** Follow each new step in red to draw this dachshund.

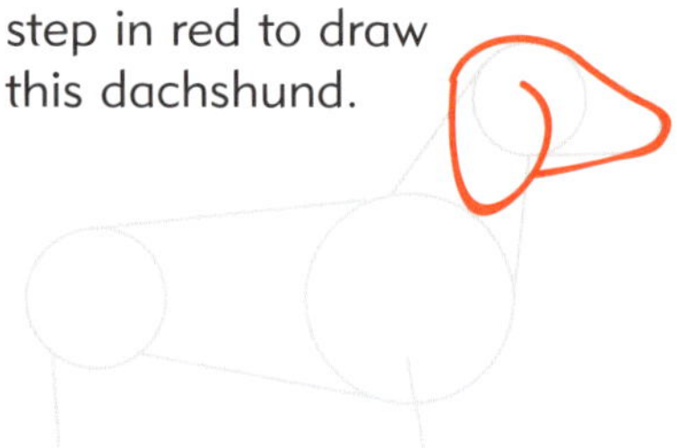

3.

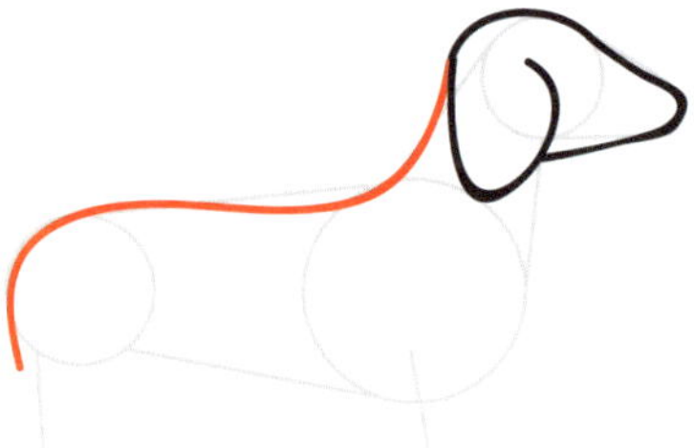

4.

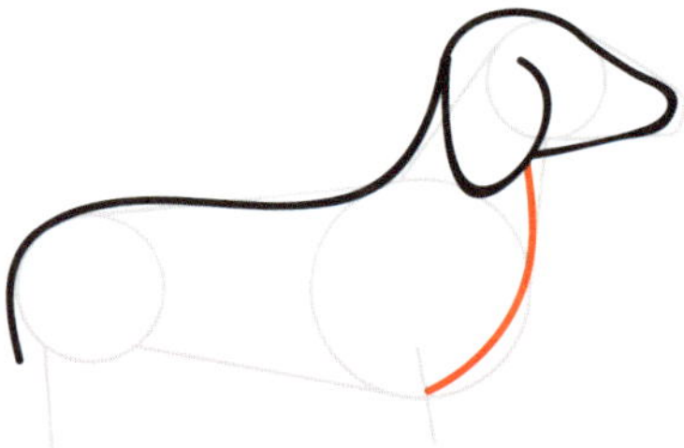

5.

6.

Trace over us
for practice!

Bunny

1.

To begin: Lightly draw these basic shapes.

2.

Then: Follow each new step in red to draw this bunny.

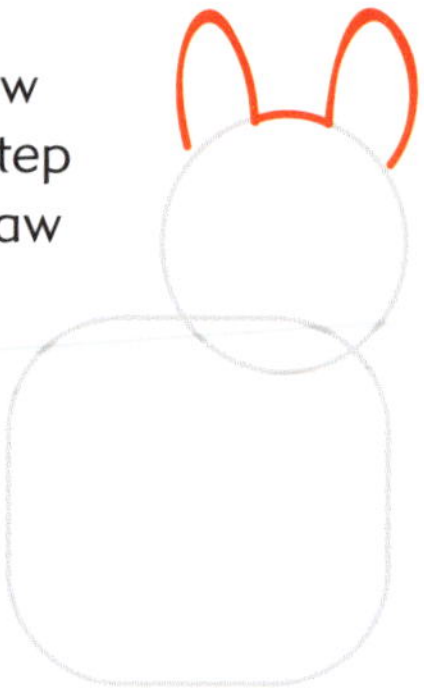

3.

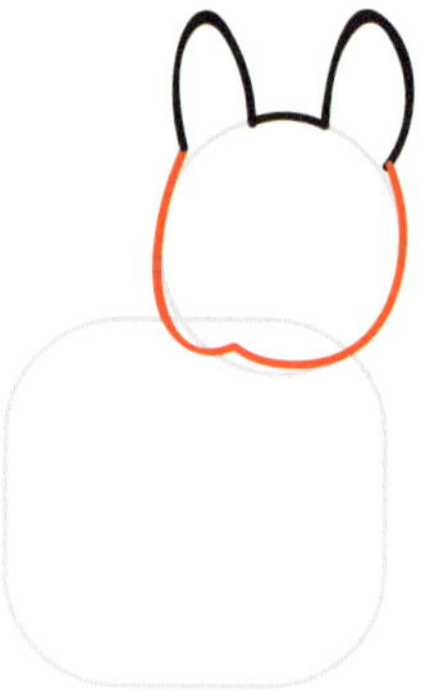

4.

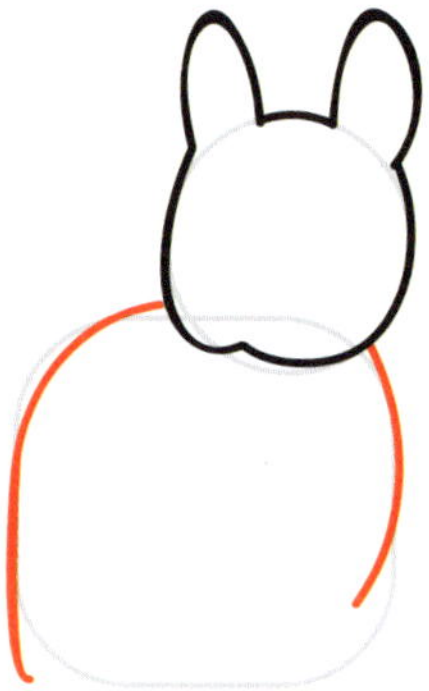

5.

6.

Rabbit

1.

To begin: Lightly draw these basic shapes.

2.

Then: Follow each new step in red to draw this rabbit.

3.

4.

5.

6.

Trace over us
for practice!

Horse

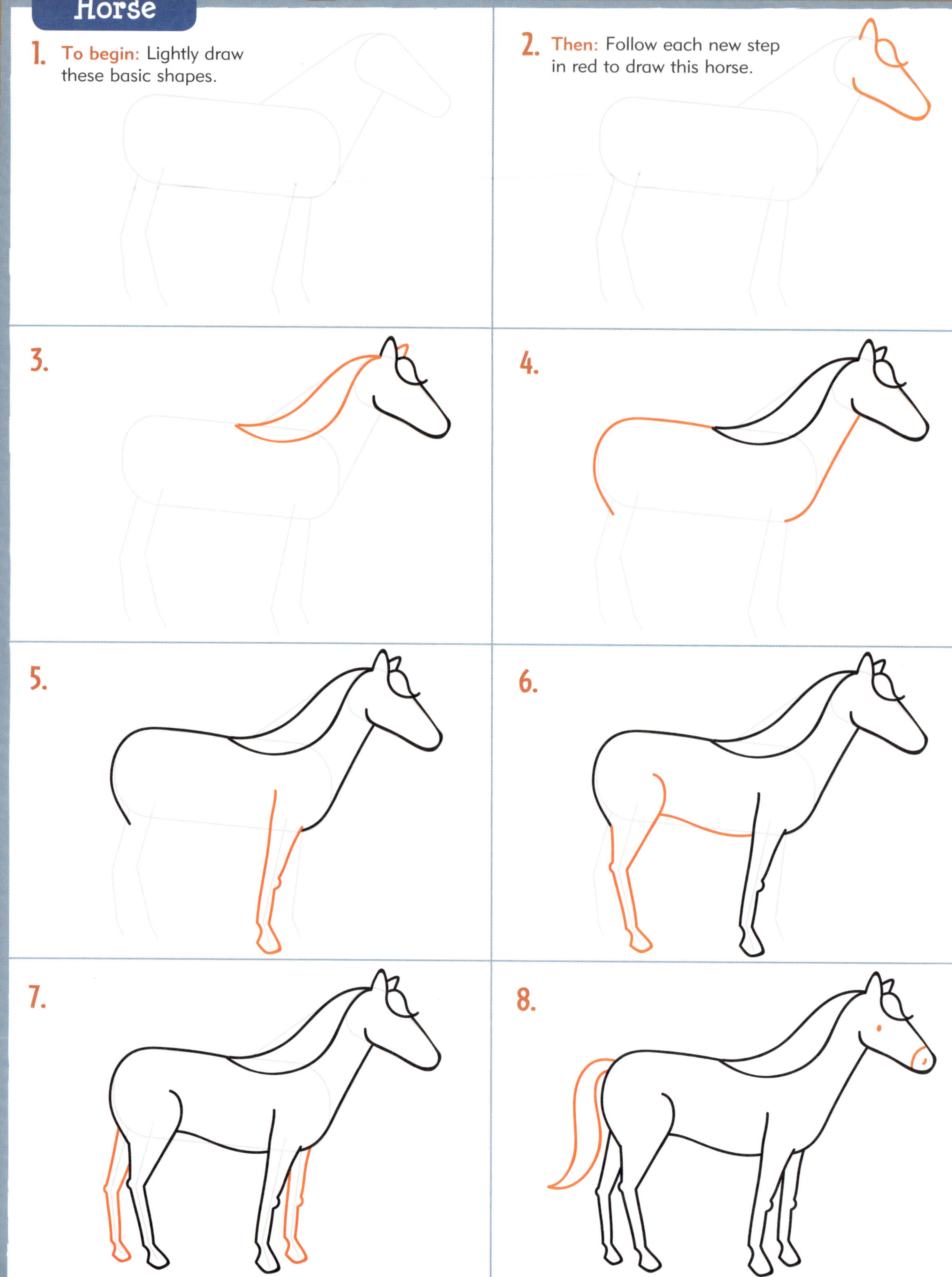
1. To begin: Lightly draw these basic shapes.
2. Then: Follow each new step in red to draw this horse.
3.
4.
5.
6.
7.
8.

Trace over me
for practice!

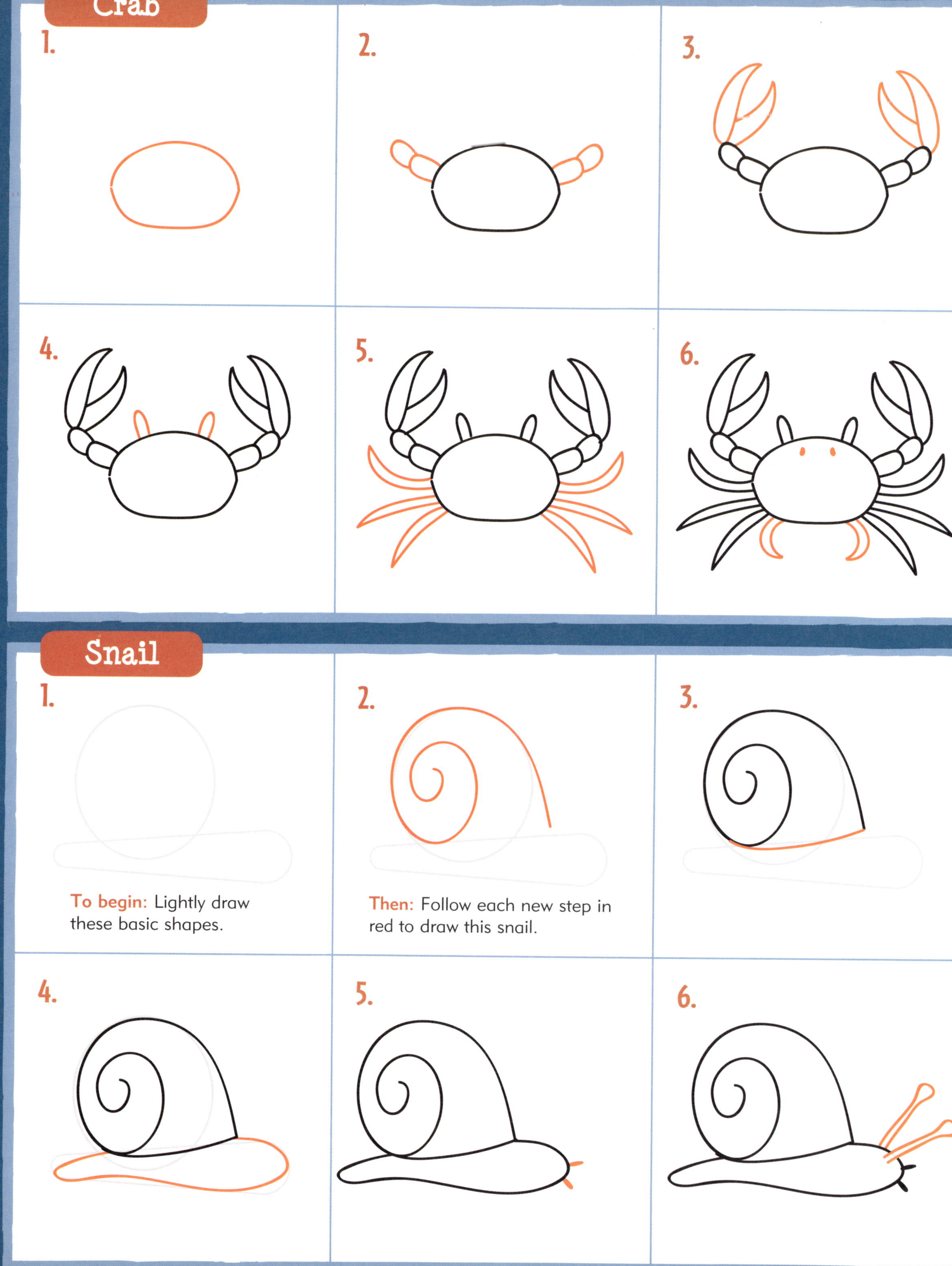
Crab
1.
2.
3.
4.
5.
6.
Snail
1.
2.
3.
To begin: Lightly draw these basic shapes.
Then: Follow each new step in red to draw this snail.
4.
5.
6.

Trace over us for practice!

Hamster

1.

2.

3.

4.

5.

6.

Gerbil

1.

To begin: Lightly draw these basic shapes.

2.

Then: Follow each new step in red to draw this gerbil.

3.

4.

5.

6.

Trace over us
for practice!

Chihuahua

1.

To begin: Lightly draw these basic shapes.

2.

Then: Follow each new step in red to draw this Chihuahua.

3.

4.

5.

6.

Pomeranian

1.

To begin: Lightly draw this basic shape.

2.

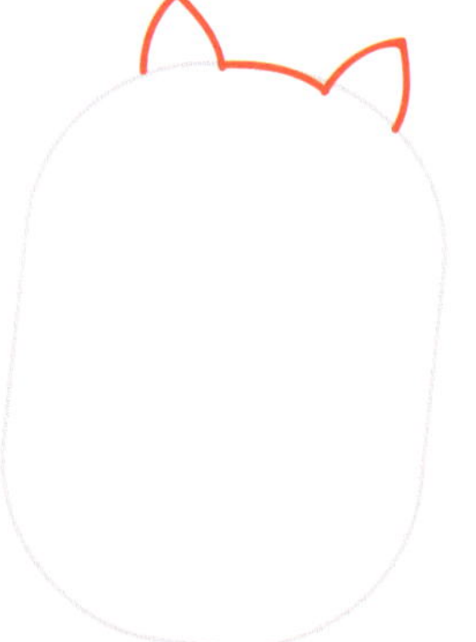

Then: Follow each new step in red to draw this Pomeranian.

3.

4.

5.

6.

Trace over us
for practice!

Tarantula

1.

2.

3.

4.

5.

6.

Snake

1.

2.

3.

4.

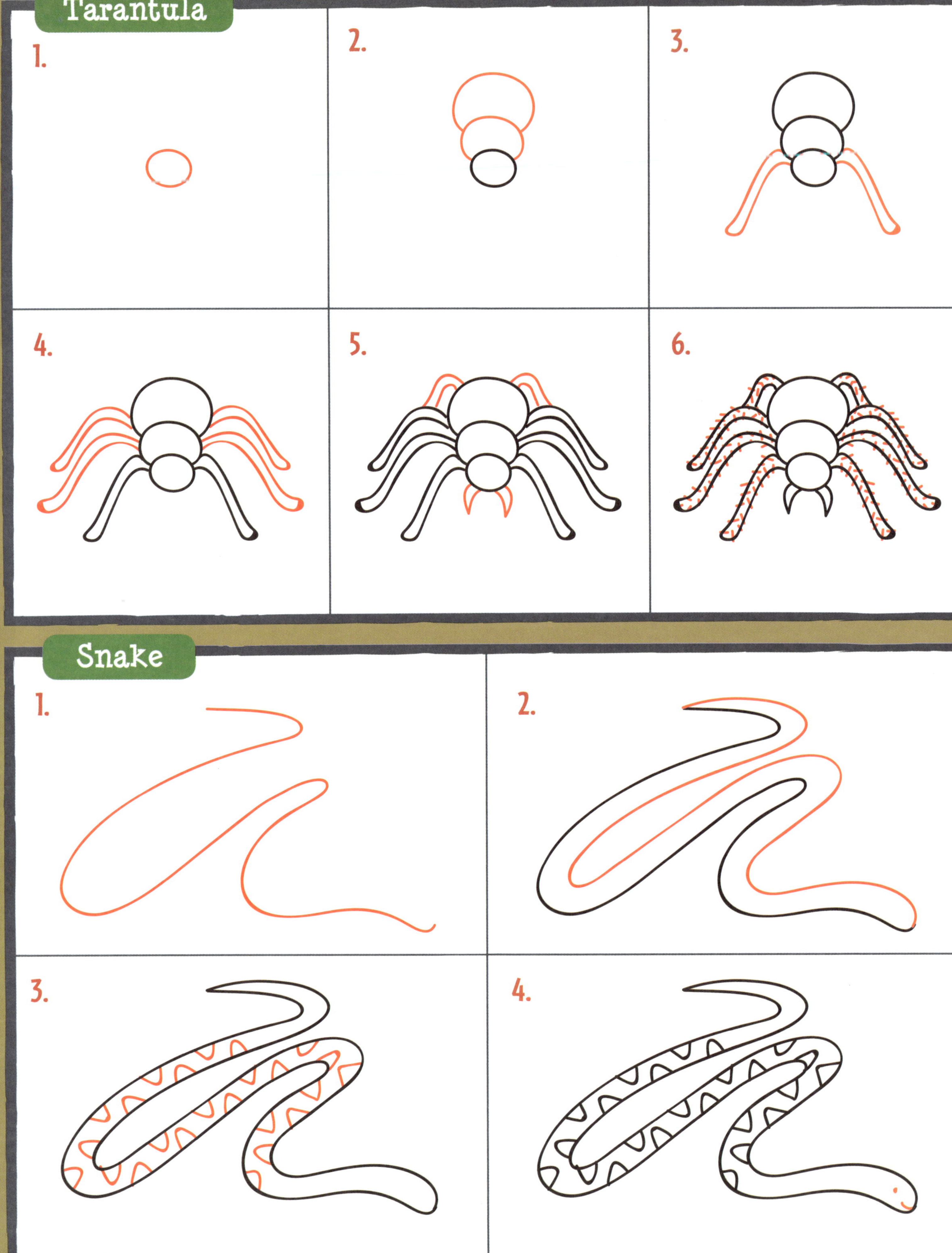

Trace over us
for practice!

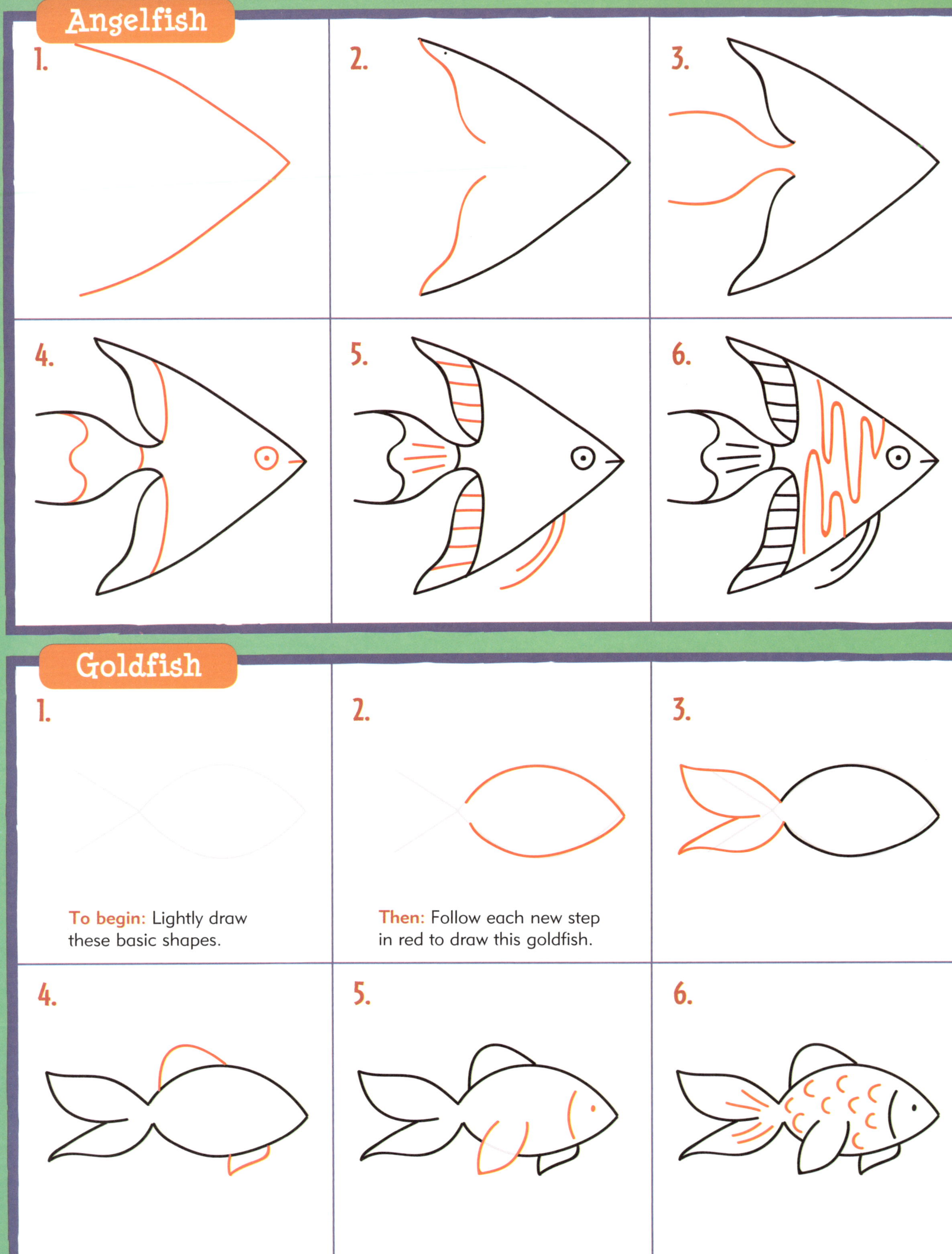
Angelfish
1.
2.
3.
4.
5.
6.
Goldfish
1.
2.
3.
To begin: Lightly draw these basic shapes.
Then: Follow each new step in red to draw this goldfish.
4.
5.
6.

Trace over us for practice!

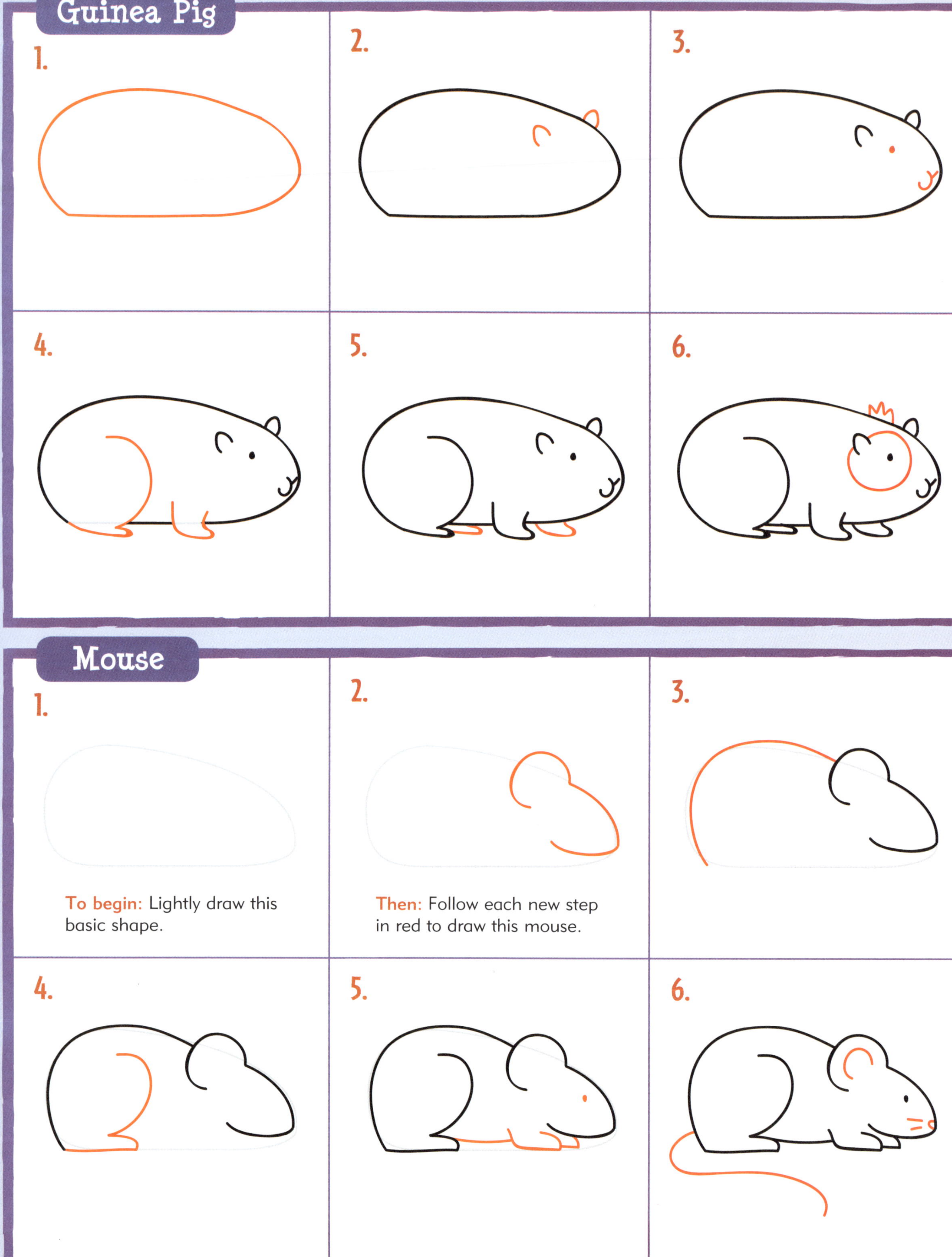

Guinea Pig
1.
2.
3.
4.
5.
6.
Mouse
1.
2.
3.
To begin: Lightly draw this basic shape.
Then: Follow each new step in red to draw this mouse.
4.
5.
6.

Trace over us
for practice!

Chick

1.

To begin: Lightly draw these basic shapes.

2.

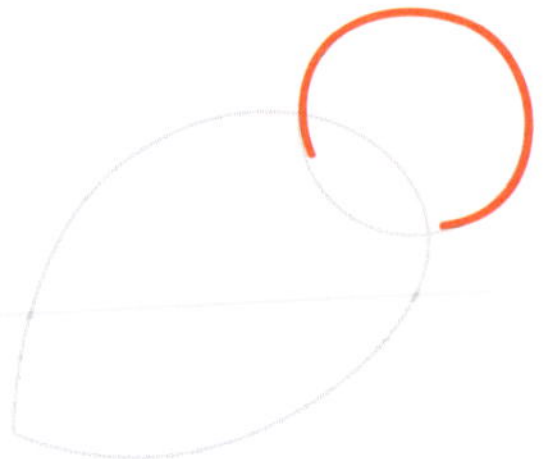

Then: Follow each new step in red to draw this chick.

3.

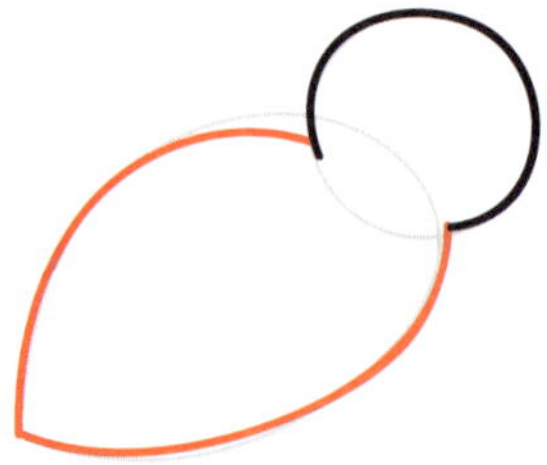

4.

5.

6.

Chicken

1.

To begin: Lightly draw these basic shapes.

2.

Then: Follow each new step in red to draw this chicken.

3.

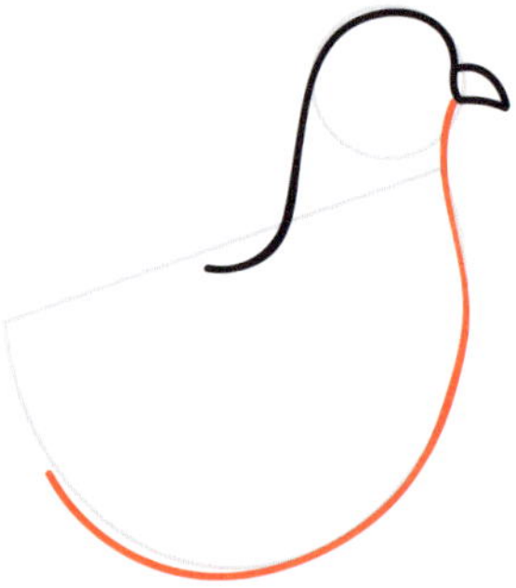

4.

5.

6.

Trace over us
for practice!

Iguana

1. **To begin:** Lightly draw these basic shapes.

2. **Then:** Follow each new step in red to draw this iguana.

3.

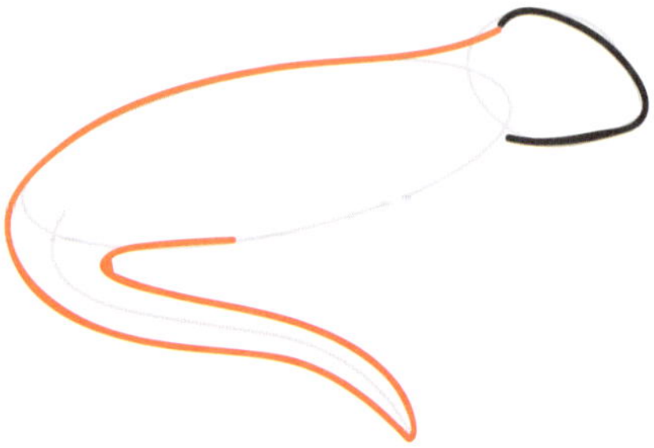

4.

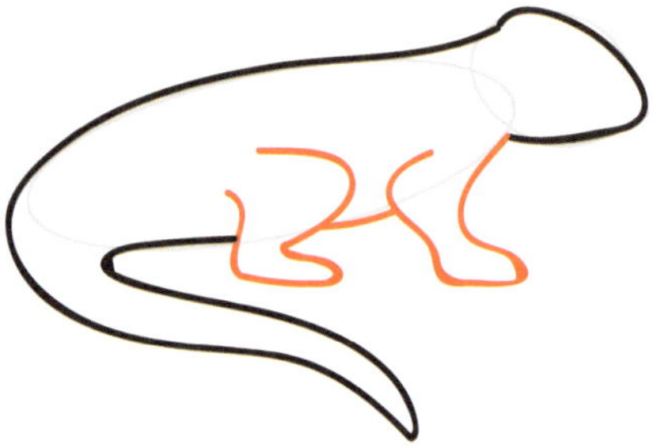

5.

6.

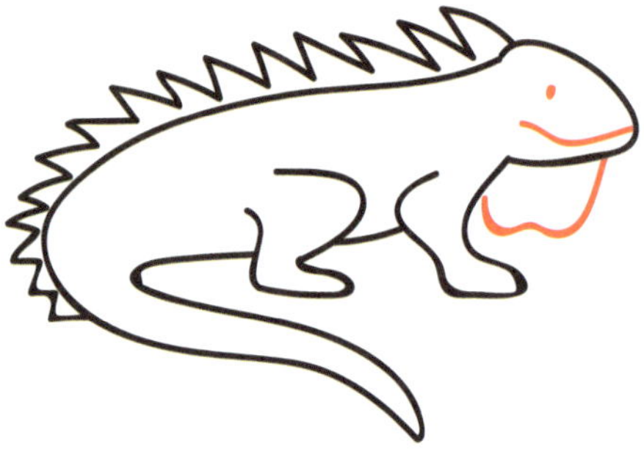

Gecko

1. **To begin:** Lightly draw these basic shapes.

2. **Then:** Follow each new step in red to draw this gecko.

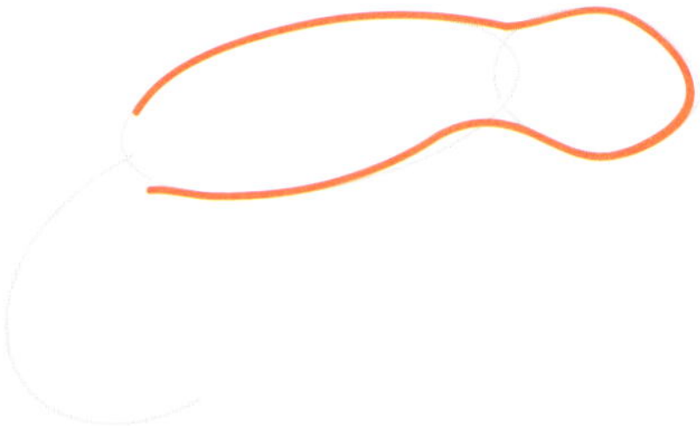

3.

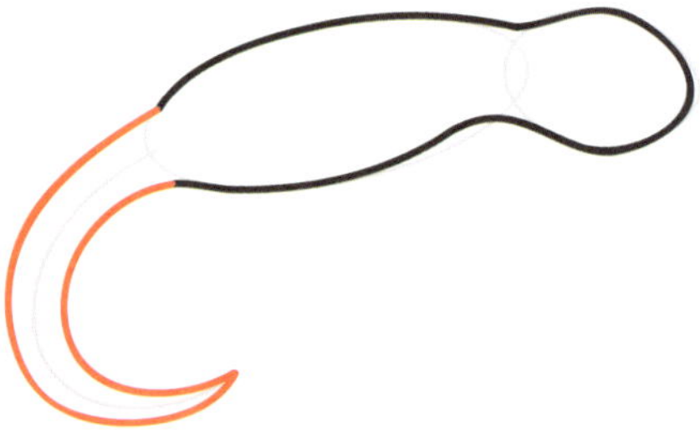

4.

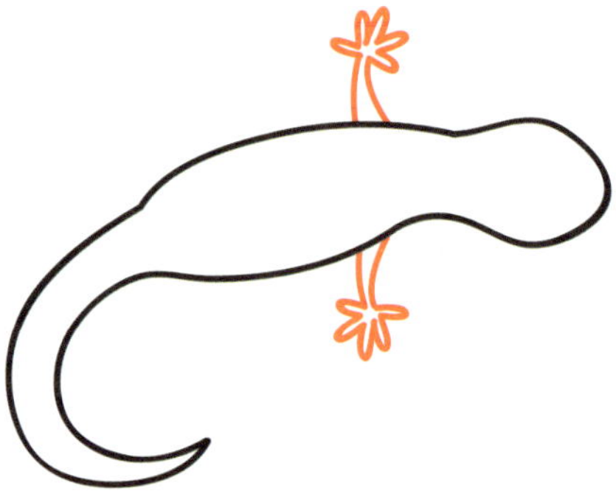

5.

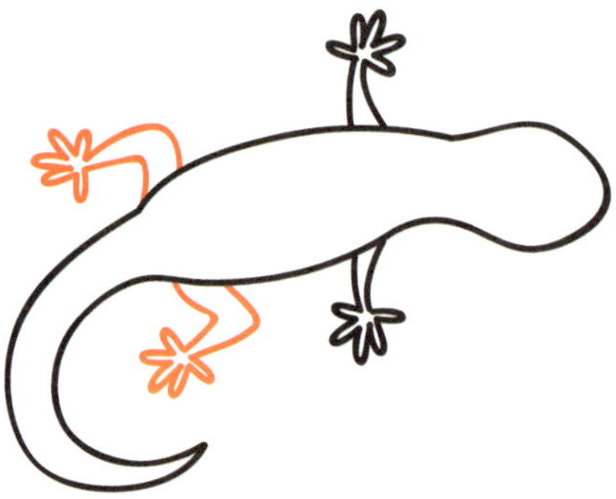

6.

Trace over us
for practice!

Flying Squirrel

1.

To begin: Lightly draw these basic shapes.

2.

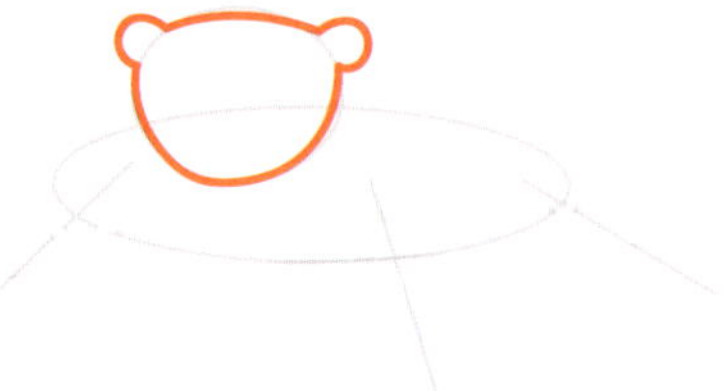

Then: Follow each new step in red to draw this flying squirrel.

3.

4.

5.

6.

Ferret

1.

To begin: Lightly draw these basic shapes.

2.

Then: Follow each new step in red to draw this ferret.

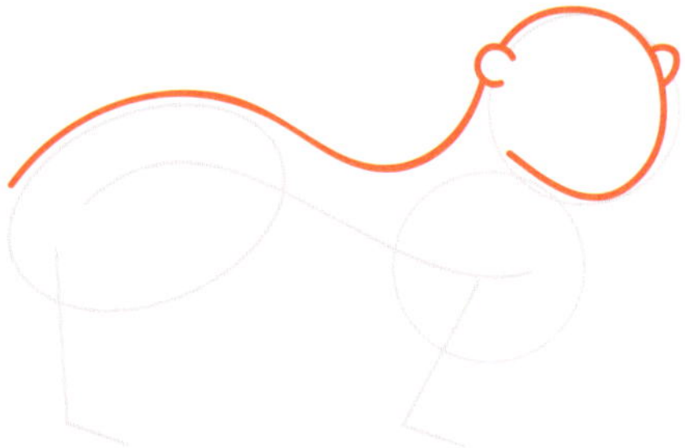

3.

4.

5.

6.

Trace over us for practice!

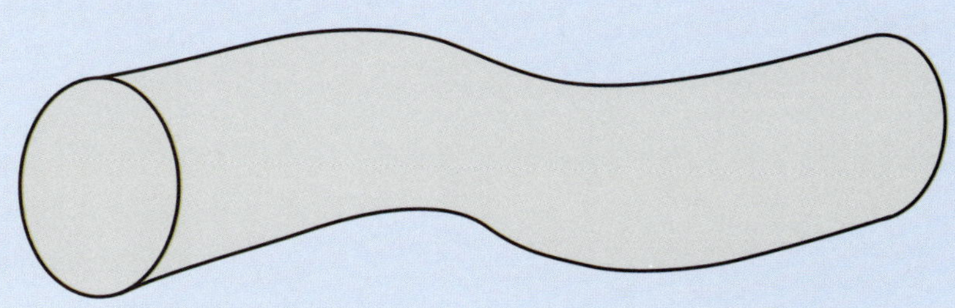

Parrot

1. 

2. 

3. 

To begin: Lightly draw these basic shapes.

Then: Follow each new step in red to draw this parrot.

4. 

5. 

6. 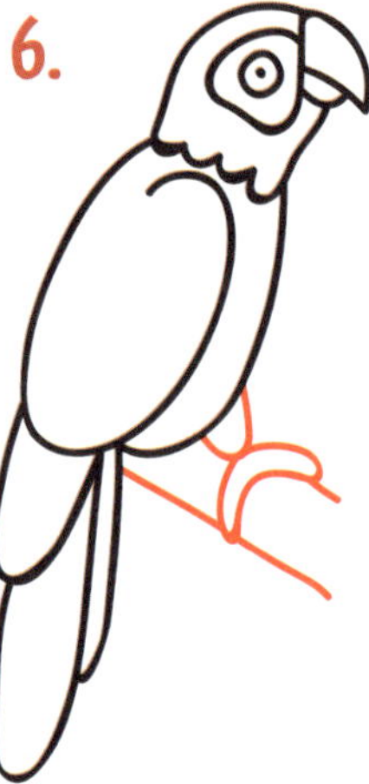

Cockatoo

1.

2.

3. 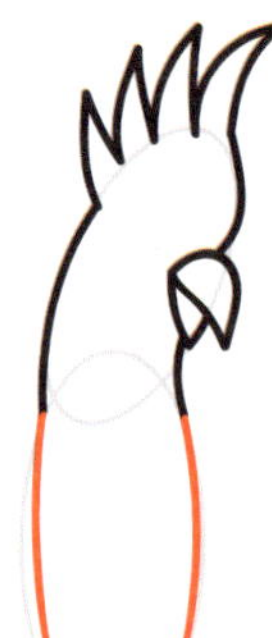

To begin: Lightly draw these basic shapes.

Then: Follow each new step in red to draw this cockatoo.

4. 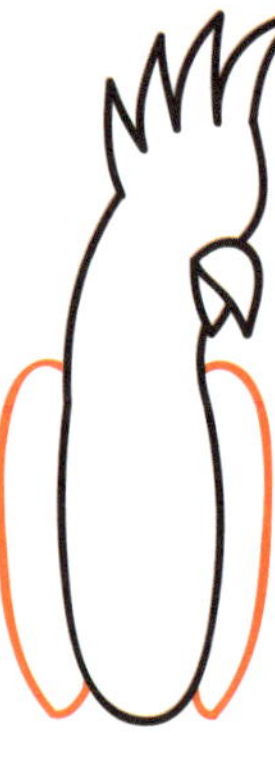

5. 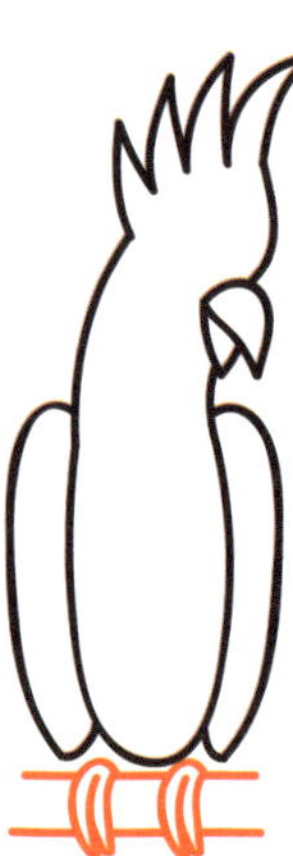

6. 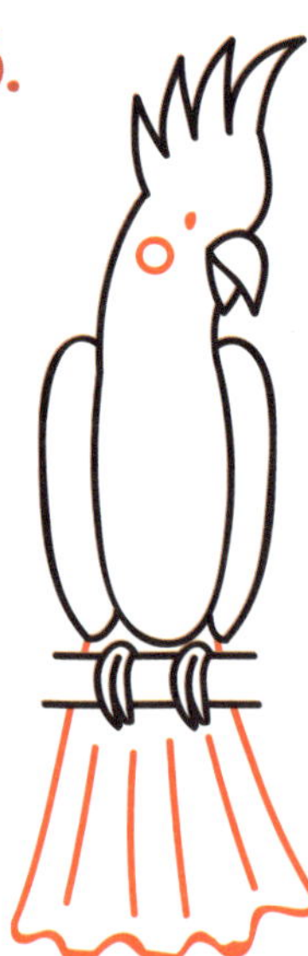

Trace over us for practice!

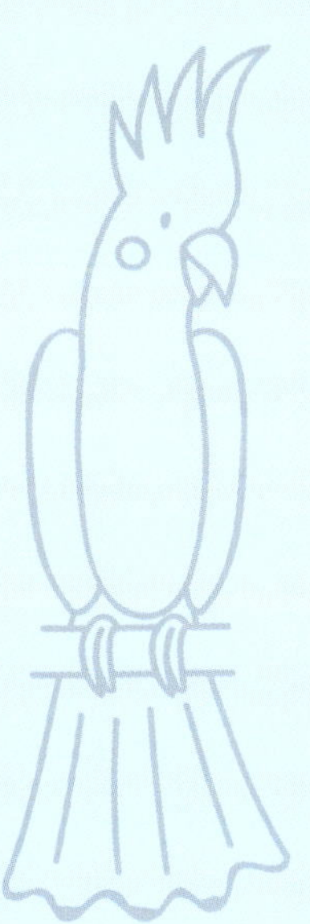

Shih Tzu

1\. **To begin:** Lightly draw these basic shapes.

2\. **Then:** Follow each new step in red to draw this shih tzu.

3\.

4\.

5\.

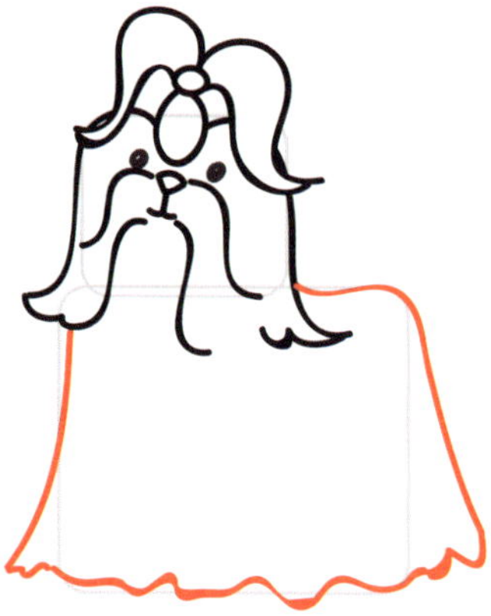

6\.

Great Dane

1\. **To begin:** Lightly draw these basic shapes.

2\. **Then:** Follow each new step in red to draw this great dane.

3\.

4\.

5\.

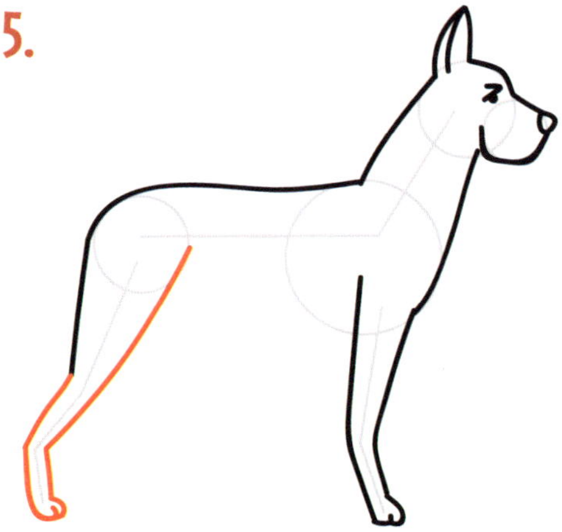

6\.

Trace over us for practice!
Dog Park

Lovebirds

1.

2.

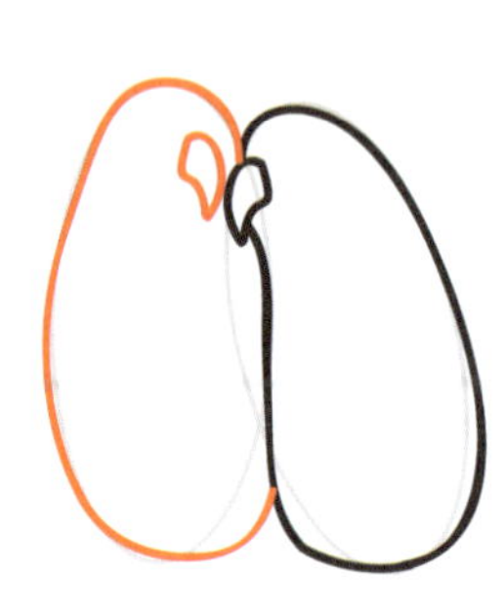

3.

To begin: Lightly draw these basic shapes.

Then: Follow each new step in red to draw these lovebirds.

4.

5.

6.

Parakeet

1.

To begin: Lightly draw this basic shape.

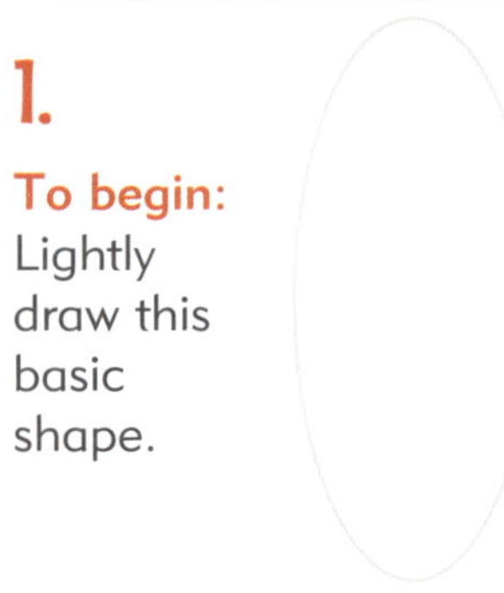

2.

Then: Follow each new step in red to draw this parakeet.

3.

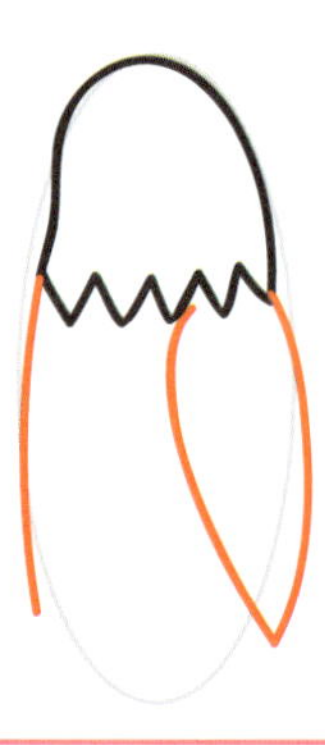

4.

5.

6.

Trace over us
for practice!

West Highland Terrier

1. **To begin:** Lightly draw these basic shapes.

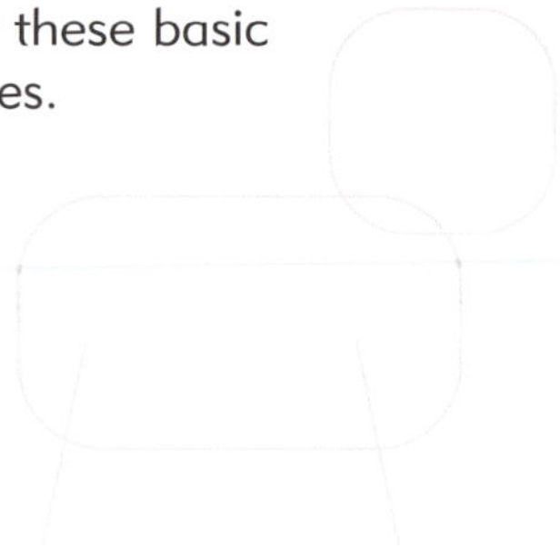

2. **Then:** Follow each new step in red to draw this West Highland terrier.

3.

4.

5.

6.

Poodle

1. **To begin:** Lightly draw these basic shapes.

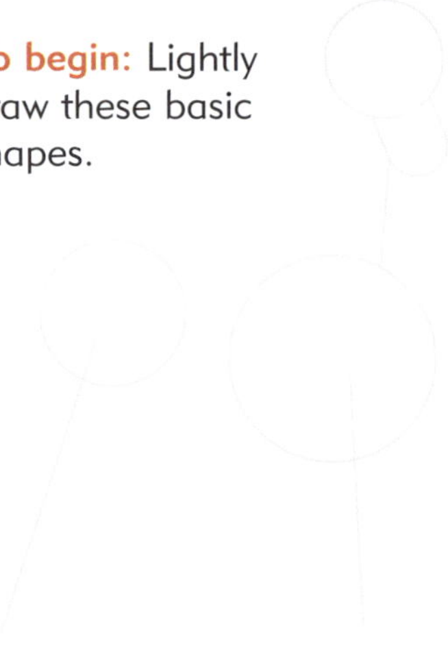

2. **Then:** Follow each new step in red to draw this poodle.

3.

4.

5.

6.

Trace over us
for practice!

Clownfish

1.

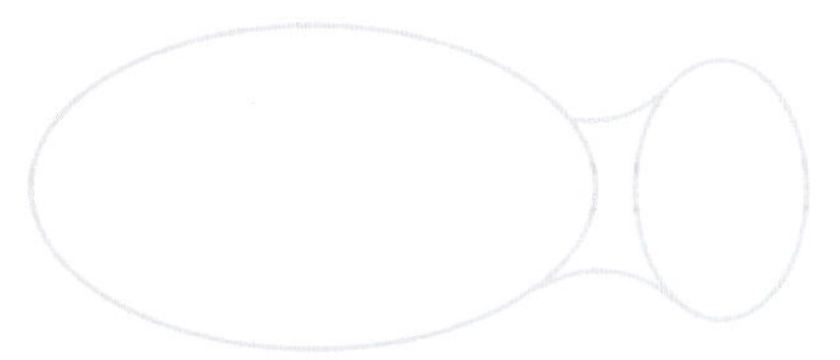

To begin: Lightly draw these basic shapes.

2.

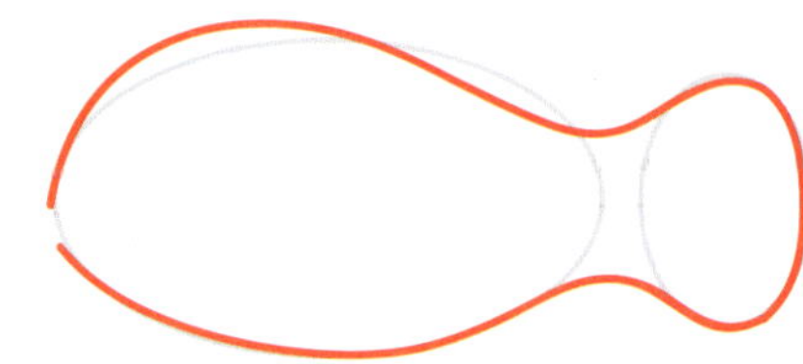

Then: Follow each new step in red to draw this clownfish.

3.

4.

5.

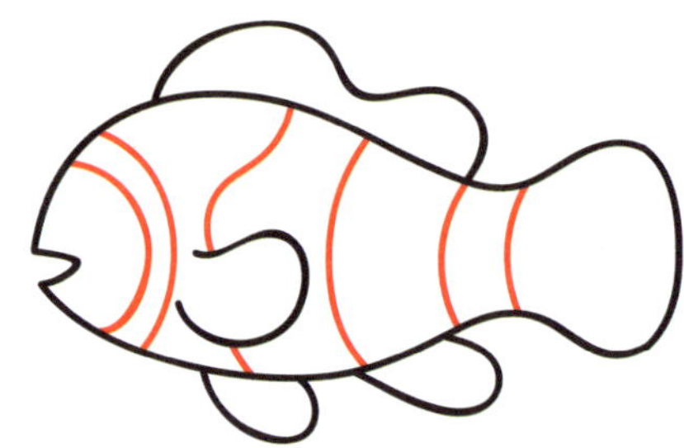

6.

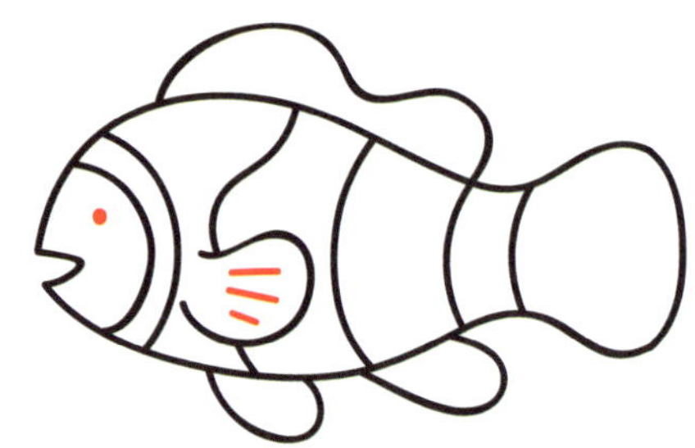

Royal Blue Tang

1.

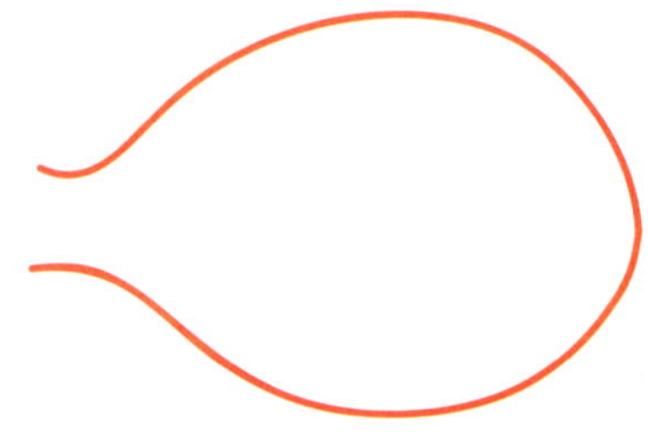

2.

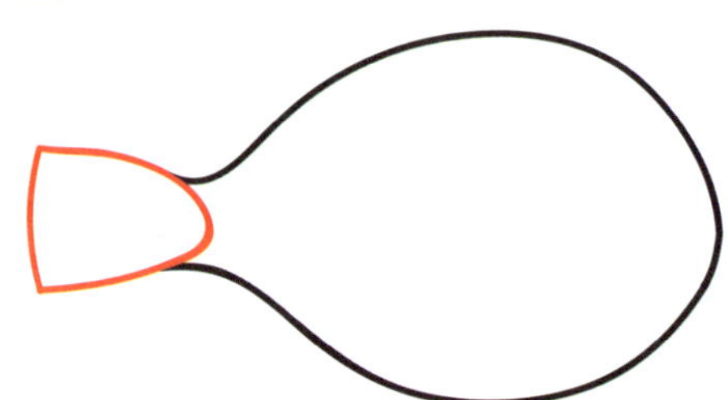

3.

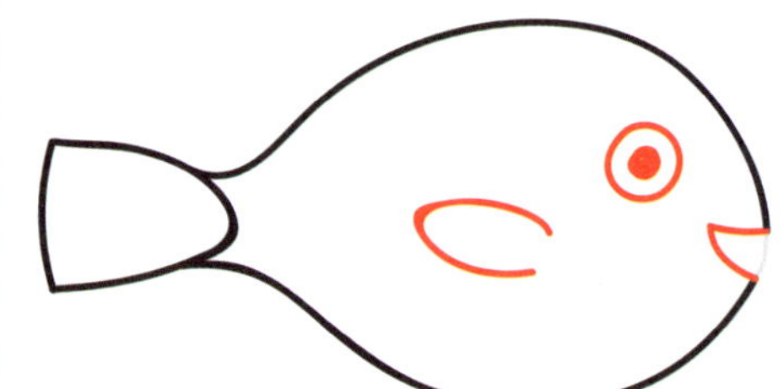

4.

5.

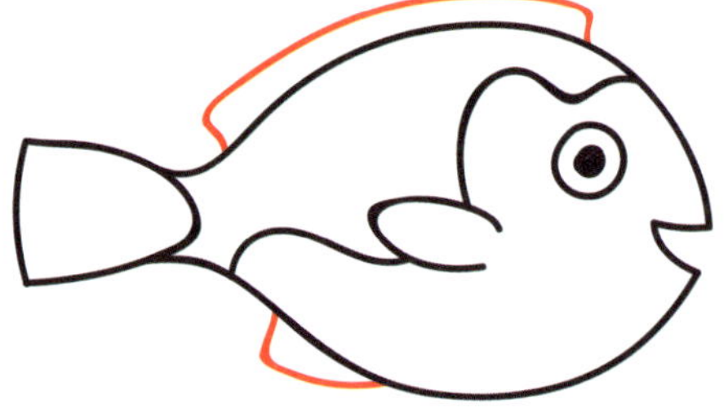

6.

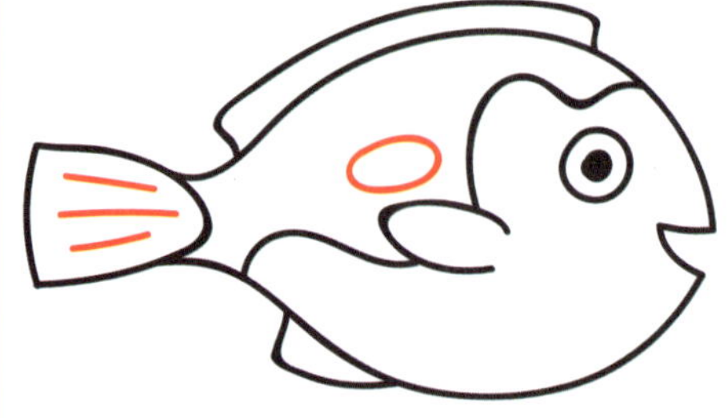

Trace over us
for practice!

Turtle

1.

2.

3.

4.

5.

6.

Frog

1.

To begin: Lightly draw these basic shapes.

2.

Then: Follow each new step in red to draw this frog.

3.

4.

5.

6.

Trace over us
for practice!

French Bulldog

1. **To begin:** Lightly draw these basic shapes.

2. **Then:** Follow each new step in red to draw this French bulldog.

3.

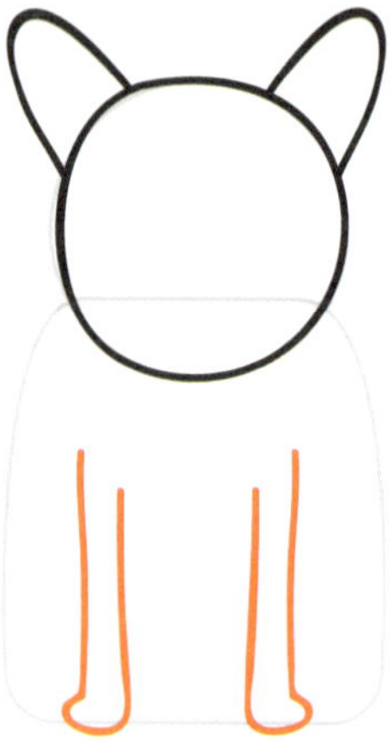

4.

5.

6.

Pug

1. **To begin:** Lightly draw these basic shapes.

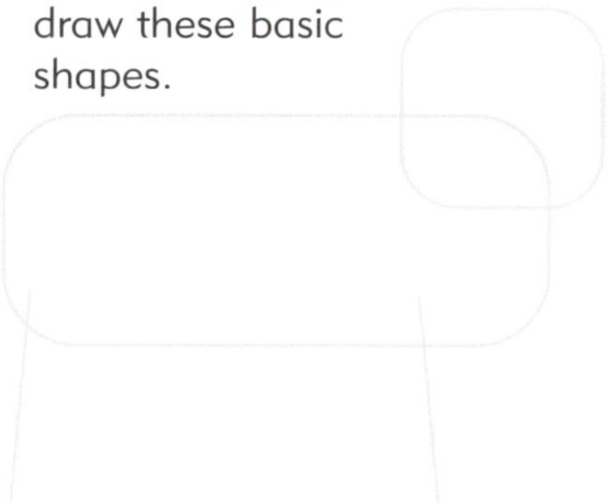

2. **Then:** Follow each new step in red to draw this pug.

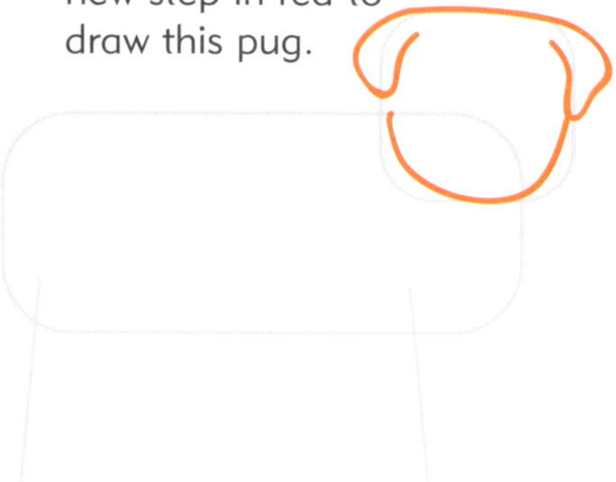

3.

4.

5.

6.

Trace over us for practice!

Pygmy Goat

1. **To begin:** Lightly draw these basic shapes.

2. **Then:** Follow each new step in red to draw this pygmy goat.

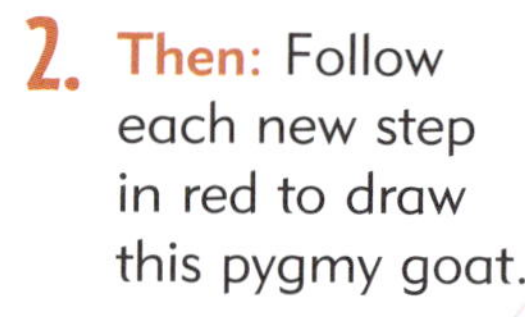

3.

4.

5.

6.

Teacup Pig

1. **To begin:** Lightly draw these basic shapes.

2. **Then:** Follow each new step in red to draw this teacup pig.

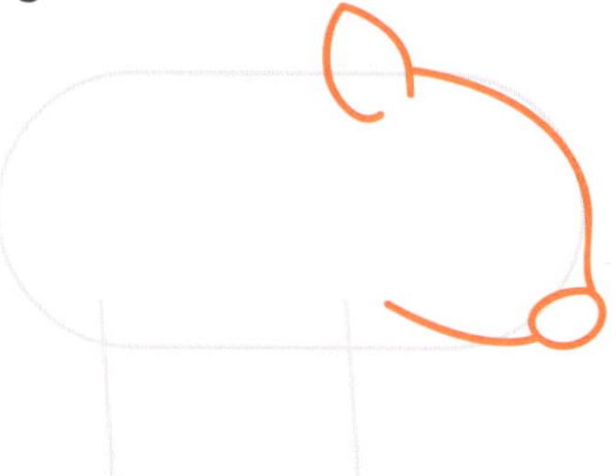

3.

4.

5.

6.

Trace over us
for practice!

Chinchilla

1. **To begin:** Lightly draw these basic shapes.

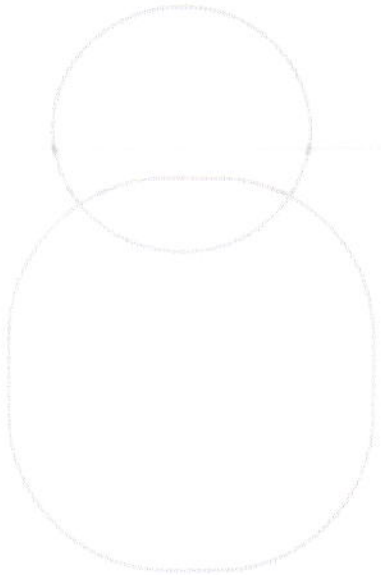

2. **Then:** Follow each new step in red to draw this chinchilla.

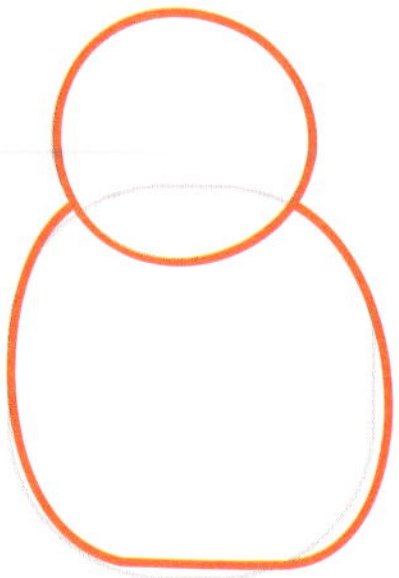

3.

4.

5.

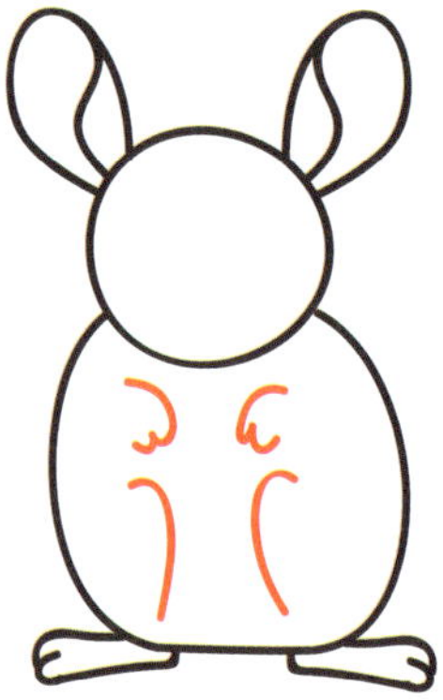

6.

Hedgehog

1. **To begin:** Lightly draw this basic shape.

2. **Then:** Follow each new step in red to draw this hedgehog.

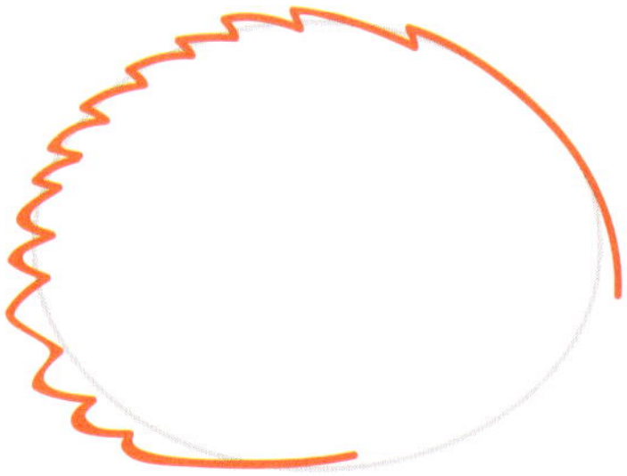

3.

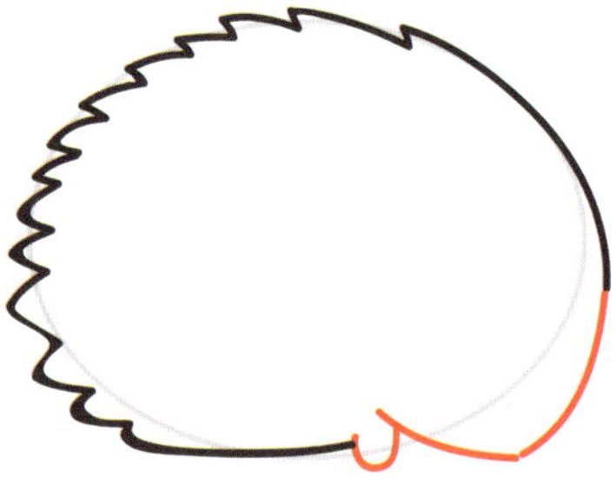

4.

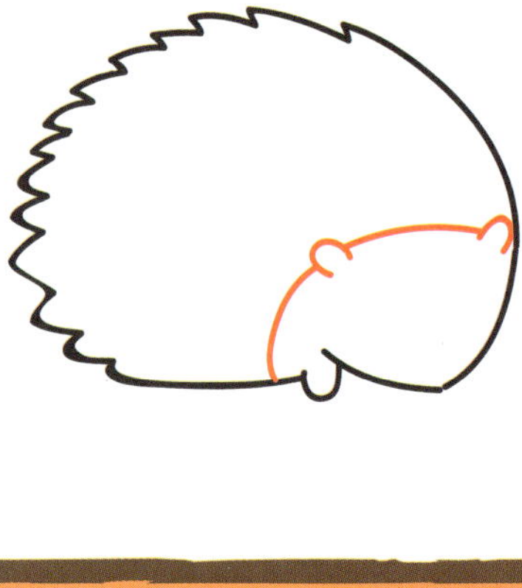

5.

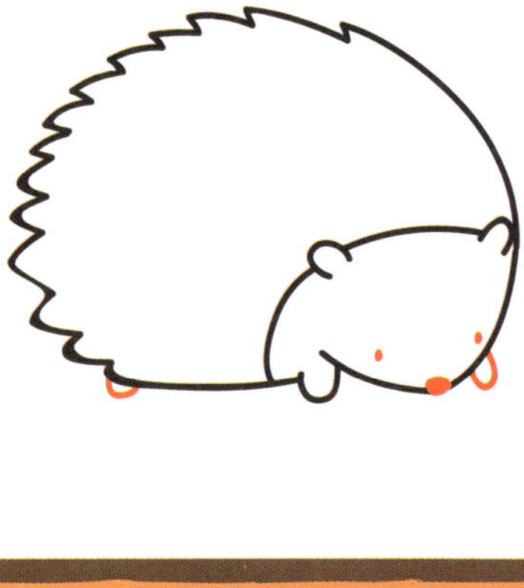

6.

Trace over us
for practice!

We've reached
the end, and now
we're done.
Playful pets
are so
much fun!